The Making of A Prophet

Women Walking In Prophetic Destiny

Kimberly Moses

REJOICE
Essential Publishing

Kimberly Moses/Rejoice Essential Publishing

PO BOX 512

Effingham, SC 29541

www.republishing.org

Unless otherwise indicated, scripture is taken from the King James Version.

Scripture quotation marked (EXB) taken from The Expanded Bible. Copyright ©2011 by Thomas Nelson. Used by permission. All rights reserved.

The Making Of A Prophet/ Kimberly Moses

ISBN-10: 1-946756-54-7
ISBN-13: 978-1-946756-54-1
Library of Congress Control Number: 2019942802

Dedication

This book wouldn't be possible without the inspiration of the Holy Spirit. This manuscript sat in my spirit for many years as the Lord downloaded it to me. He gave me the blueprint and I just obeyed as I wrote the manuscript.

2 Timothy 3:16-17 says, "All scripture is given by inspiration of God, and is profitable for doctrine, for reproof, for correction, for instruction in righteousness: That the man of God may be perfect, thoroughly furnished unto all good works."

This book is for all the women prophets who are hiding in the cave and for women who want to walk in destiny and purpose.

This book, "The Making of A Prophet: Women Walking In Prophetic Destiny," is a Godsend. The Lord has filled a mighty void with this book. The book brought even more clarity to the calling within my life. Being a person called to the office of a prophet and having no understanding of what a prophet was, I can relate to the personal stories within the book. Over the last year, I've felt crazy and lost, but just as Kimberly Moses stated in the book, "We are not crazy just prophetic." There were no prophets around me when I was called. However, it wasn't long after asking God to direct me to a prophet that He called.

Then I found Prophetess Kim's books. This book fills the first mandate of acceptance to the call and direction. It answers the who am I, what am I, and how to function preliminarily as a prophet questions. It removes the questioning of why me. It also helps the young prophet to remove doubt and accept the calling before them. Everything in this book will bring comfort and open your understanding of your call. Although the book is directed toward women, it is relatable to anyone. I will be buying a few to share with some young prophets that I know who just received their call to the office. If you have read any of her books this one is just as powerful if not more powerful than all others because you can see her heart for the young prophetess. — Zolisha L Ware

***

What a beautiful compilation of testimonials about modern day women prophets! The gift of prophecy is a gift from Jesus created and personified by Prophetess Moses in this book. She gives delightful details and steps for the new woman prophet.

Many women can identify with Prophetess Moses. She is a perfect example because she normalizes the process to see their delightful and wonderful gift from the Lord. Please obtain the book or take her course. Prophetess Moses is very passionate and will pray for you. She will put you on the right path toward this beautiful calling from the Lord.— Phyllis Tanks

***

In this time, there are many women prophets on the rise. Prophets hear the voice of God and are sensitive to His timing. True prophets don't draw people to themselves. They always point people to God. Prophetess Kimberly is a true prophet of God. When the Lord speaks through her, just like the prophet Samuel, her words never fall to the ground. 1 Samuel 3:19 says, "The LORD was with Samuel as he grew up, and he let none of Samuel's words fall to the ground." She has spoken into my life and mentored me in the School of Prophets. Those words manifested immediately.

The calling comes with warfare and the wilderness experience. It is not a strange thing happening. It is for our good. Prophetess Kimberly has endured much, but it only sharpened the gift in her. We must be pruned for the work. He must cut away all that is not like Him. This book will show you how to allow God to take you through the process. It will teach you how to walk in your calling as a prophet and tell you her story of surrendering to the process of the anointing on your

life. This book will forever change your life! —
Yolanda Samuels

***

This book is very informative. It will teach
you about all the women prophets. This book is
a great tool to come against the wrong teachings
that women should not be preachers. You will
learn that God calls true prophets. I really love
Prophetess Kimberly's testimony and her journey to becoming a prophet. This book is a must
read. —Kentia Middleton

***

This book is powerful. As I read it, I felt God's
fire and presence. I began to pray right in the
middle of reading it when a burden of intercession hit me. I was encouraged as I read about the
women God used in the Bible. I realized that I
might have been rejected, but God will always
make time for me, like the woman at the well.
Prophetess Kimberly Moses' encounters with

God and testimonies inspired me as well. Thank you, Prophetess, for your transparency. Your honesty makes you relatable. This book has anointed scripture-based teaching. It is a thorough teaching on Women Prophets that left me falling more in love with Jesus and His righteousness. —Tijuana Killian

***

Thank you, prophetess Kimberly Moses, for taking your time out to write this book on the women prophets. It blessed me and still is blessing me. I loved when you said, "That many people think that God can't use them because of their past." Many women are slandered in the gospel. As they read this book, it will encourage them. You mentioned, "Women are discriminated against because of their background," I felt like you were talking directly to me which helped me to walk confidently in my call as a prophet. Thank you, Prophetess Kimberly, for your obedience to the Holy Spirit. May the grace of God keep you and your family. — Tammy Crenshaw

***

This book is sent by God. I have heard so many times how women cannot prophesy, teach, or preach due to their lack of anointing. God can use anybody to deliver and execute His divine plan. Prophetess Kimberly, the Lord has used you in such a mighty long way; even I can quote Bible verses with an explanation. God's Glory is felt on from start to finish. God's Word will go forth this time, season, and hour of manifestation. —-Leslie Harvey

***

I have watched and listened to many teachings on the prophetic. I have not come across a teacher who has more Biblical foundational truth about the office of the Prophet, especially as a women prophet. At this hour as the Sons of Issachar were anointed to know the times and season in the spirit, Prophetess Kimberly Moses has a timely book for women in the prophetic. Her teaching will train you and open your eyes to the revelation of the word of God regarding the prophetic. This is a bold and rare book about women in the prophetic. If you are a woman or man who wants more wisdom on the role of the prophet for both genders, this book will be a key for your knowledge expansion on this neglected topic in the body of Christ. I can attest that Prophetess Kimberly Moses, is a great teacher and experience through accurate prophecies. She has spoken in my life from the first time that I watched one of her LIVE teachings. Her books and teaching are for this time and the coming era in the Prophetic across the global. —- Farah Jackson

***

I enjoy reading books by Prophetess Kimberly Moses. She's an amazing teacher of the Prophetic Ministry and an asset to the Body of Christ. This book will enlighten your understanding of the Women Prophets in Biblical times and help you to understand what women Prophets of today are dealing with. It will bring clarity of your own identity as a Prophet of God. I used to feel left out and different from the rest, until I found people that were just like myself. Her books are filled with wisdom; the knowledge you obtain from her books will stick with you. I had the pleasure of taking her course "School of the

Prophets," which was life-changing for me. I encourage anyone looking to fulfill the prophetic call on your life to take her course. You will never be the same. — Felecia Jackson

***

This book is very necessary! Women are misunderstood not only throughout the world as far as equality, but women are misunderstood when it comes to God's purpose in their lives. God mandated everyone, Male or Female, with a purpose. I'm so glad that this book described Biblical women that God uses continually throughout the Word of God, but also powerful testimonies from the writer, Prophetess Kimberly Moses. Being a student of the School of Prophets, Prophetess Kimberly imparts to her students, and we began to flow in dreams, visions, Word of knowledge, Word of Wisdom and increase of discerning of spirits. Her Love for people and God shows and is all in the fruit God does through Prophetess Kimberly. This book will bless you! — Anstrice Mcmillian Epps

***

"The Making of A Prophet: Women Walking In Prophetic Destiny" is a must read! When I started reading the first declaration, I could feel the fire of God, so I knew this book was anointed. Some of the declarations in this book are declarations that I either already speak or have spoken over myself, and there are other declarations in this book I felt were for me. I also appreciate Prophetess Kim's testimonies in this book. The transparency she displays is encouraging because just like so many others (including myself), Prophetess Kim did not see herself as being worthy enough to used by God, especially as a prophet. When God called Prophetess Kim to the office of a prophet, she felt that she was in a terrible state in her life but being in that state was how she was able to trust and rely on God. When Prophetess Kim finally surrendered to God, He was able to use her more for His glory.

"The Making of A Prophet: Women Walking In Prophetic Destiny" is truly a blessing for me because it gives me the encouragement and boldness that I need to move in the prophetic without focusing on the distractions or objections from others who disagree with women operating in their God-given assignment. People will try to put limits on you, but when it comes to God, there are no limitations; Prophetess Kim makes that clear in this book. She challenges and breaks the barriers some people try to use against women operating in church, ministry, five-fold offices, etc.

"The Making of A Prophet: Women Walking In Prophetic Destiny" will inspire you to move forward in your assignment with the confidence in knowing that God has you, He is with you, and you have what it takes to carry out His purpose for your life, with or without the approval of others. Thank you, Prophetess Kim, for allowing God to use you to bring this much-needed book forward, blessings to you always!— LaShana Lloyd

***

Contents

Acknowledgments

To Zolisha Ware, I appreciate your love and support. You are the mentee that I always wanted. I don't take for granted to be able to impart into your life. The fruit of the Holy Spirit that I see from our connection is beyond words. You are talented, smart, and anointed. I'm excited about the plans that God has for you. I love you.

To Phyllis Tanks, I am humbled that a powerful woman of God as yourself came underneath my ministry. You are full of wisdom and hard working. You made the "School of the Prophets," easy for me. I appreciate all the love, support, and kindness that you have shown me. I am amazed at how the Lord activated you in the word of knowledge. I will never forget that night during class because it made all the warfare worth it which is to impact a life.

To Yolanda Samuels, you are truly a woman that walks by faith not by sight. You are one of the few people that I know that will labor in fasting and prayer to obtain their promise from the

Lord. You motivate me to believe God for the miraculous. Over a short time, I saw how the Lord had brought one promise after another to pass in your life. You are a great role model for women. It's incredible to be able to connect with people who want to go higher in God. Thank you for all the love and support. I love you.

To Kentia Middleton, I am so proud of you. I am blown away at how much you have grown. You are strong and loyal. Thank you for believing in the vision that God has given me. Thank you for having my back when the enemy tried to attack me. Thank you for your prayers and support. I will never forget that. Good people are hard to come across, but you are one of them. Thank you for allowing me to mentor you. I love you. I can't wait to see you graduate and walk in all that God has for you.

To Tijuana Killian, I appreciate your support and your labor of love. I'm grateful that the Lord connected us. I always wanted to be around a company of intercessors. God answered that prayer when He allowed us to connect. You encourage me as I watch you persevere through the warfare. I see a lot of myself in you. I am grateful that I met you during the beginning stages because one day, the Lord will make your name great. Thank you for allowing me to mentor you, I don't take it lightly.

To Tammy Crenshaw, your love and zeal for God are infectious. You always stir up the gifts that the Lord has placed on my life. You are a great example of what promotion looks like. It's incredible to see you operate in the word of knowledge and healing. I love how the Lord allowed me to impart into your life. I am so proud of you and glad to be your mentor. I have seen you overcome every obstacle that was set before you. It's encouraging to see because I know that you will have every promise. You are truly unique; please don't ever change. I love you and keep going forward.

To Leslie Harvey, thank you for always being faithful. You are one of the strongest intercessors on, "Tongues of Fire," prayer call. I look forward to praying with you during our 6 a.m. calls. It great to be able to connect with others who love God just as much as I do. Thank you for supporting my ministry and allowing me to impart into you. Thank you for allowing God to use you during the "Prayer-A-Thon." I love how the Lord is getting you out of your comfort zone because you are going higher. I appreciate you.

To Farah Jackson, thank you so much for allowing me to be your mentor. You made teaching the "School of the Prophets," easy for me. You always came to class hungry and ready to learn. You truly know how to put a demand on the anointing. I appreciate your love and support. You are a woman of strength, courageousness, and love. I know God will bless you with all your heart's desires. Thank you for being meek and teachable. I bless God for you.

To Felecia Jackson, you are a strong woman of God. I witnessed the warfare that you endured and how the Lord blessed you victoriously. Thank you for allowing me to impart into your life. Thank you for taking the correction and not getting offended at me. Thank you for helping me with proofreading this book. Thank you for your prayers and support. I enjoyed the prayer call that we did in the "School of the Prophets."

Once you got stirred up, you were on fire. Please don't ever lose that fire but continue to fan it to keep it burning.

To LaShana Lloyd, your work ethic is supreme. You walk in the Spirit of Excellence. You realize the value of the things of God, and I appreciate that about you. I love your professionalism and your love for God. I thank God for our connection. I appreciate your sacrifice and your labor of love. You are what I needed for my ministry to be more effective. I am forever grateful. Thank you for allowing me to mentor you and impart into your life. I look forward to fellowshipping and laboring together in the Kingdom. I love you.

Introduction

Are you called to the prophetic and have a lot
of questions? That's how I was when I first was
called. I had so many questions and was very misunderstood. No one was around that could help
or teach me about the prophetic. When I told my
leaders everything that was happening to me at
the time, they thought I was crazy. I didn't receive
clarity about my call until God revealed to me the
reason why I was experiencing supernatural encounters. You may be called to the prophetic and
you may have a lot of questions. Numbers 12:6

says, "And he said, Hear now my words: If there be a prophet among you, I the LORD will make myself known unto him in a vision, and will speak unto him in a dream." That scripture gave me peace and brought insight into my destiny.

God is raising up women in this season as never before. God has anointed His daughters to do great exploits in the earth. You may have a tremendous anointing on your life and can prophesy. However, we need to be knowledgeable of the prophets in the Bible, so we can relate to someone. Prophets are prone to rejection and loneliness. The enemy loves to attack them emotionally. If prophets aren't careful, they will feel like they are the only one left or going through something (1 Kings 19:10). Many prophets have experienced the same or similar trials that you may be experiencing (Matthew 5:12). To stay encouraged on this journey, prophets must know and understand Biblical prophets.

We will cover false prophets and true prophets of God. You will be empowered to walk in your prophetic destiny and be able to relate to one of these women in the Bible. We will discuss the women that God used in the Bible and challenges that women around the world face. We will demystify the scriptures used against women preachers by breaking it down. God uses women, and He wants to use you too. Also, I will share my testimony of how God called me as a prophetess and some of the challenges that I faced. Lastly, there are anointed declarations that you can say daily to strengthen you as you walk in all that God has for you.

CHAPTER ONE

Declarations

I am anointed by God.

I am highly qualified for what God is calling me for.

I will face every challenge head on in the name of Jesus.

I am God's handiwork (Ephesians 2:10).

I will be confident in the things that God is calling me to do.

God has already equipped me to complete the assignment.

I will not get intimidated by the faces of people.

I will set my face like a flint (Isaiah 50:7).

I will cry aloud and spare not (Isaiah 58:1).

I will not back down from the threats of the enemy.

I will walk in all that God has for me.

I will be like a roaring lion speaking, "Thus saith the Lord."

The Lord will fill my mouth with His words.

I will not fear in the name of Jesus.

I decree and declare a hedge of protection around me.

I decree longevity in my prophetic ministry.

I decree and declare that my ears are open to hear the still small voice of the Holy Spirit.

I decree and declare that the Lord will order my steps.

I decree and declare I am highly anointed and favored by God.

I decree and declare that the Lord is the lifter of my head (Psalm 3:3).

I decree and declare that I will speak all that the Lord gives me to speak.

I decree and declare that I will no longer hold back to please people.

I decree and declare I will no longer be afraid to prophesy to someone that has a title.

I decree and declare that I will no longer be afraid of what people think or say.

I decree and declare that I will be as bold as a lion of Judah (Proverbs 28:1).

I decree and declare that out of my belly will flow rivers of living water (John 7:38).

I decree and declare that I have the mind of Christ (1 Corinthians 2:16).

I decree and declare that my thoughts are subject to Jesus Christ.

I decree and declare that I will no longer be confused between the voice of God, the voice of the enemy, or my voice.

I decree and declare that I have eyes to see in the spirit realm.

I decree and declare that my eyes are sharp and keen to see what the Holy Spirit wants me to see.

I decree and declare that I will not operate in divination in Jesus name.

I decree and declare that I will not get side-tracked by operating in the flesh, the pride of life, or in the lust of the eyes.

I decree and declare that I will use this gift to glorify God and Him only will I serve.

I decree and declare that the only words spoken out of my mouth will edify grace unto the hearers (Ephesians 4:29).

I decree and declare that the words out of my mouth will glorify the Lord God.

I decree and declare that God will give me confidence and comfort when I must give hard prophetic words.

I decree and declare that I will no longer hold back in Jesus name.

I decree and declare that the Lord speaks through my mouth.

I decree and declare that the Lord gives me words of wisdom out of my mouth.

I decree and declare in the hour when I don't know what to say the Lord speaks through my mouth.

I decree and declare that the Lord will give me the counsel to minister unto His people.

I decree and declare that the Lord orders my steps.

I will always be in the right place at the right time.

I decree and declare that all the spiritual gifts on my life are increasing powerfully in Jesus name.

I decree and declare that I will fan the flames of my spiritual gifts that were imparted to me by my spiritual leaders or the Lord (2 Timothy 1:6).

I decree and declare that I will shun evil and run far from it (Proverbs 14:16).

I decree and declare that I will not use my gifts for my own selfish gain.

I decree and declare that I will not misuse the gifts that God has placed upon me.

I decree and declare that the motives of my heart will be right before I do something.

I decree and declare that every snake in the grass is removed out of my life.

I decree and declare that every snake in the grass is removed out of my life.

I decree and declare that I will be obedient to God no matter what the cost.

I decree and declare that I will step out of my comfort zone so I can grow spiritually in Jesus' name.

I decree and declare that I will have a long life. No devil in hell will stop what God is going to do through me and inside of me in Jesus' name.

I decree and declare that any Jezebel spirit coming against my life dies by the fire of the Holy Spirit.

I decree and declare that no weapon formed against me shall prosper in the name of Jesus (Isaiah 54:17).

I decree and declare that God will give me strength in times of weariness.

I decree and declare that God will give me peace in times of chaos.

I decree and declare that I'm in tune with the Spirit of God.

I decree and declare that I'm going to be in God's timing for my life.

I decree and declare that I'm sensitive to the presence of God.

I decree and declare that I am a carrier of the glory.

I decree and declare that I hear the voice of God clearly.

I bind up the enemy from speaking to me in Jesus' name.

I decree and declare that God has given me strategies to walk with Him.

I decree and declare that wealth and riches are in my house (Psalm 112:3).

The prophetic anointing creates lots of wealth in my life.

I decree and declare that the prophetic anointing causes me to be prosperous in all areas.

I decree and declare that my gifts are making room for me and bringing me into the presence of great men.

I decree and declare that I am emotionally sound.

I decree and declare I will be led by the Spirit of God and not my emotions.

I decree and declare that I am a friend of God.

I decree and declare that the secrets of the Lord belong to me because I fear him (Psalm 25:14).

I decree and declare that I will walk circumspectly (Ephesians 5:15).

I decree and declare that I will pray about everything and everyone that wants to connect to me in Jesus' name.

I decree and declare that God is giving me a great circle of people that are loyal, dependable, and trustworthy in Jesus' name.

I decree and declare that God will surround me with people that are not jealous of me but support me.

I decree and declare that God will align me with people that are in tune with my destiny.

I decree and declare that God will anoint all my projects and everything that I'm called to do.

I decree and declare that God will send me to the nations.

I decree and declare that God will cause my voice to be amplified in the earth.

I decree and declare that anything resisting me breaks in the name of Jesus.

I decree and declare every muzzle that's on my mouth falls to the ground in Jesus' name.

I decree and declare that none of the words that I've spoken will fall to the ground.

I decree and declare that I have a supernatural grace for fasting and intercession.

I decree and declare that I am a demon buster in Jesus' name.

I decree and declare that God is using me as a weapon of war (Jeremiah 51:20).

I decree and declare that I am the Lord's battle ax (Jeremiah 51:20).

I decree and declare that God is going to use my mouth for His glory.

I decree and declare that the word of God coming out of my mouth is like fire (Jeremiah 23:29).

I decree and declare that the word of God coming out of my mouth is like the hammer that breaks the rock in pieces (Jeremiah 23:29).

I come against the spirit of rejection in Jesus' name.

I come against the spirit of the delay in Jesus' name.

I come against the spirit of stagnancy in Jesus' name.

I come against attacks on my destiny in Jesus' name.

I come against demonic strongholds and entanglements in Jesus' name.

I come against demonic chatter and snakes in the grass.

Lord, pour fresh oil upon on my mantle.

Anoint me with the oil of gladness.

Protect my life from all harm and danger in Jesus' name.

Lord, let every witch, warlock, and agent of Satan that is sent to come against my ministry die by the fire of the Holy Spirit.

Lord, order my steps and always cause me to be in Your will.

Lord, allow me to pay attention to the red flags and not get caught up in words of flattery.

Lord, show me the hearts of people so I can know the intents of men's heart.

Lord, always reveal to me what's on your heart.

Lord, bless me to be consistent in prayer and fasting.

Lord, let me be a good student of the word.

Lord, let me study to show myself approved unto you.

Lord, let me be a good steward of your mysteries.

Lord, let me walk in the grace and not get out of the grace that you have assigned to me.

Lord, let my ministry be effective and be productive.

Lord, expand my territory for your glory.

Lord, give me an anointing to gather a mighty harvest for your glory.

Lord, give me an anointing of deliverance.

Give me an anointing for healing.

Give me an anointing for the word of knowledge.

Give me the anointing for the gift of working of miracles.

Give me an anointing for the gift of discerning spirits.

Give me an anointing for the gift of faith.

Give me an anointing for the word of wisdom.

I prophesy that all spiritual gifts are activated and working at the full capacity in Jesus' name.

I prophesy that I will stay humble and stay in the prayer closet.

I prophesy that whatever I do privately God will bless me openly.

I prophesy that I love the Lord with my whole heart, soul, and mind. I love His people as I love myself.

I prophesy that I will be faithful in my assignment.

I prophesy that I will hunger and thirst after righteousness.

I prophesy that I will connect to people that are living right and that are serious about the things of God.

I prophesy that I will not judge people about the same things God delivered me out of.

I prophesy that I will serve others with the gifts that are on my life.

I prophesy that the Lord will take my ministry far and wide.

I prophesy that the hand of the Lord is upon my life.

I prophesy that I will not grieve the Holy Spirit.

I prophesy that I have a burden for prayer and intercession.

I prophesy that I will finish every assignment that the Lord has given me to finish.

I prophesy God will use me to do great things in the lives of people that are connected to me.

I prophesy that I am a deliverer in the name of Jesus.

I prophesy that the Lord will raise me up out of the pit into the palace.

I prophesy that I have the full armor of God on.

I prophesy that every attack against me is canceled.

I prophesy that all word curses are returning to sender.

Lord, use me for your glory.

Lord, anoint and favor the ideas you have given me.

Lord, use me to anoint your people.

Lord, use me to impart into your people.

Lord, use me to encourage your people.

Lord, give me more knowledge of who you are.

Lord, visit me and show me your glory.

Lord, give me a visitation with your son Jesus.

Lord, give me angelic visitations.

Lord, let me feel your fire daily.

Lord, I can't live without your presence.

Lord, I can't do this without you.

Lord, you are the vine and I am the branch. Apart from you, I can do nothing.

Lord, purge me and prune me.

Take me through the sanctification process.

Lord, let me decrease, and you increase in me.

Lord, let me win souls for your glory.

Lord, expand my territory for your glory and your kingdom.

Lord, give me favor with people of influence so I can tell them about Jesus.

Lord, raise people up with your heart.

Lord, let your will be done on earth as it is in heaven.

Lord, use me to bring your glory down on this earth.

I prophesy that God will use me in the miraculous.

I prophesy that the anointing on my life is increasing.

I prophesy that I walk in signs and wonders.

I prophesy that I will have precision and prophetic accuracy.

I prophesy that my relationship with God is increasing.

I prophesy that God will use me in a new way that my generation has never witnessed before.

I prophesy greater works I will do than what Jesus did.

I prophesy that my faith is going to another level so I can prophesy according to the proportion of my faith.

I prophesy that I will not blurt things out.

I prophesied that I will not release a word out of season.

I prophesy that I will not perform to people please.

I prophesied that I will walk in destiny and purpose.

I prophesy that I will never use my gifts for the enemy.

I prophesy that I will grow spiritually each year.

Lord, do a work in my heart, soul, and mind.

I prophesy that I will be a pure vessel for your glory.

I prophesy that I'm being transformed more into the image of Jesus Christ.

I prophesy when people see me, they'll see Jesus Christ.

I prophesy that I will walk the way Jesus walked.

I prophesy that I will talk like Jesus talked.

Lord, I will speak when you tell me to speak, and I will be silent when you tell me to be silent.

CHAPTER TWO

My Testimony

When I reflect on how my life took a dramatic shift within a short time frame, I am amazed. I had everything going for myself. I owned a home in my mid-twenties, drove a nice SUV, had top credit, and so much more. On the outside, it seemed like everything was perfect but on the inside was a pending storm. I was on the brink of divorce and didn't know it. During this time, I was saved but only went to church out of routine, yet my heart was hard towards the things of God. I was very carnal and continued to be a friend of the world. For ten years, I sat in church and didn't want to serve or grow spiritually.

My life was falling apart, and I wasn't even aware of it. In 2013, my children's father moved us to Colorado because of a job transfer. It was supposed to be a fresh start for us, but we ended up divorcing a few months of arriving. I was devastated, and I acted out in rage. I destroyed some property and ended up on probation for two years. Since I was on probation, I couldn't leave the state. I began to have financial hardship, and I hit rock bottom. I was broken, scorned, and tormented by the enemy. I looked around, and I was mad at myself for being that foolish woman that tore down her house.

I was experiencing severe anxiety which debilitated me. It was difficult to function and do daily tasks. I went to counseling, and it provided some relief, but the anxiety was still present. I took the prescribed medication, but the effects of the withdrawal made me feel worse than before I took the drugs. I hit a breaking point. I was tired of being depressed and living a defeated life. I decided to call out to God. I repented for backsliding. I repented for the reckless decisions that I previously made. I was hopeless, but at that moment, I started to feel the peace of God. I realized that I lost His peace over an amount of time due to sin and carnality.

When I cried out, "Lord, help me! I'm sorry for all my sins! Please forgive me! I'm tired, and I can't keep living this way anymore," God answered. Immediately, God began to shift my life. He ordered my steps by guiding me to the right scriptures and the right sermons on how to get delivered from fear. I began to meditate on the word of God and fast. The Holy Spirit inside of me started to get stronger and the enemy became weaker. Initially, the devil that was tormenting day and night started to resist my deliverance process. The devil whispered in my ear, "I hate you. I will kill you. You will die of a terrible disease. When you leave out of the house, you will get in a car accident. Reading the Bible will never work. Fasting doesn't work. Stop what you are doing now, or you will be sorry!"

I started to speak back, "Satan, I just read in the Bible that you are a liar. Fasting and reading the Bible is working." I was determined, and I became unstoppable. The devil realized that I was serious, and I wasn't going to back down. I submitted myself unto God, and the devil had no other choice but to flee. I realized who Jesus truly is and the identity that I have in Him. During this time, God began to show me how to pray and when I would ask Him a question, He would speak back. At that time, I didn't realize it was the Holy Spirit speaking to me. I thought it was my thoughts.

Over time, I discovered it was God, and when I did, the Holy Spirit took over. I started to hear the voice of God instead of the enemy. I was going through the hardest trial of my life, and I would lay on the floor for hours praying. I wouldn't eat much, and I weighed 105 pounds. I couldn't get enough of prayer, and I needed God because I lost everything. I lost my marriage, my sense of security, my home, my freedom, my dreams, and more. The only thing I knew was to pray and hear the Lord speak to me because it provided me comfort. One day I was praying about marriage restoration, I heard the Lord say, "You're a prophet." I ignored it and then I heard the Holy

Spirit repeat it. I got up from prayer because I was turned off. I didn't know what a prophet was, and I certainly didn't want to be one. I thought a prophet was an obese Caucasian man with a beard. Due to ignorance at the time, I thought there were no women prophets. "How can I be a prophet? I don't have anything to offer! Doesn't God see that my life is a mess? Why would God use someone like me?" Those thoughts flooded my mind.

As I got up from prayer, I heard, "9, 27." I was confused. "Why would God speak to me numbers and not tell me what they mean?" I told a lady what happened shortly after and she gave me a link to a website called, "God's Arithmetic." As I looked up 9 and 27 my mouth dropped opened. I saw the words, "the gift of prophecy." Since I didn't listen to the Holy Spirit directly, He told me indirectly that I was a prophet. I went back into prayer and started to receive instructions. I was so lost and had so many questions. The Lord began to minister to me about the plans He had for my life and destiny.

I was still in awe that the Lord was serious and that He chose me. I remember being in church and the spirit of prophecy would fall upon me. "Tell my people that I am doing this or that." I thought, "No way God. I'm not saying that! People will think I am crazy." Immediately, a burden or an invisible heavy weight would drop down upon my chest. It was so uncomfortable, but I was stubborn. I tried to fight God and resisted Him every time He told me to speak. The intensity of the burden would increase, and I couldn't take it anymore, so I finally obeyed Him. As a result, the burden lifted, and my heart was filled with peace. I repeated this cycle about eight times and realized that God was serious. He wasn't playing around with me, and I could no longer do what I wanted to do.

Everywhere I went, the Lord had me prophesy to everyone. During this time, the Holy Spirit instructed me to start a weekly prayer line, and I would prophesy for hours. People were amazed at how God was using me, and the prayer line grew as well as my social media presence. I was going through so much, but I decided to become serious about my walk with Jesus. I didn't want to be that carnal Christian anymore. The Lord gave me a gift, and I didn't want to mishandle it. I began to have visitations from the Lord Jesus Christ.

THE SON OF MAN

One day when I was praying, God revealed Himself to me. At the time I had no idea that this was Jesus who I saw because I never read the Book of Revelation due to fear of end-time prophecy. I saw this man with white hair and a white face that was full of light. I couldn't make out his face, but I saw that he had flaming red eyes. Then I saw something stick out of his mouth. It was a long sword, and it was so long that it scared me. This man was dressed in all white and had feet like bronze.

I became frightened and opened my eyes, and the man disappeared. I asked the Lord who was the man. He spoke to me that it was the son of man and I've seen His glory. I had no clue about what I just saw. Then a few hours later, I was led by the Holy Spirit to read the Book of Revelation. I came across these scriptures in Revelation 1:13-16, "and in the midst of the lampstands one like a son of man, clothed with a long robe and with a golden sash around his chest. The hairs of his head were white, like white wool, like snow. His eyes were like a flame of fire, his feet were like burnished bronze, refined in a furnace, and his voice was like the roar of many waters. In his right hand he held seven stars, from his mouth came a sharp two-edged sword, and his face was like the sun shining in full strength."

THE CRUCIFIXION

On October 21, 2014, I was praying with my prayer partner, and God used me to pray for her eye to be healed in Jesus' name. She had pink eye, and it cleared up after prayer. Afterward, Jesus revealed Himself to me. I saw him being crucified on the cross right before my eyes like a movie screen. I could see how bloody He was. There were many cuts and bruises upon His body. I began to feel the fire of God in my hands on the exact places where the nail prints were embedded in His hands. I felt the fire of God on the top of my feet in the exact location where the nails were in His feet. I fell to my knees and began to weep.

I saw how the Roman soldier used a spear to pierce Jesus' side. Then I saw Jesus' spirit come out of His body. Then I saw someone take Jesus off the cross and wrap him in linen. It was as if I was looking through the eyes of Mary. She was at the tomb of Jesus looking for His body. Then I saw an angel appear to her saying, "The one you seek has risen, and you can't find the living among the dead."

The scene shifted, and we were in the clouds. I spotted Jesus walking towards me. He was no longer bloody. He wore this white garment and glowed. Then I looked down at my hands, and instead of seeing my hands, I saw the hands of Jesus. It was like, Jesus was inside of me. He came up to me as He crowned my head with a crown and placing a purple robe on me. After the vision lifted and I regained my composure, I wondered, "God why did You show me this?" Then I came across this Bible verse in Galatians 2:20 (ESV), " I have been crucified with Christ. It is no longer I who live, but Christ who lives in me. And the life I now live in the flesh I live by faith in the Son of God, who loved me and gave himself for me."

ACCESSING THE THRONE ROOM

On October 22, 2014, I began to pray to God. I created an atmosphere of worship to invite the presence of God so I could continuously fellowship with Him. I had a revelation about how to access the throne room of God. I begin to read my bible and read Hebrews 4:16 (ESV) that says, "Let us then with confidence draw near to the throne of grace, that we may receive mercy and find grace to help in time of need."

I realized that this scripture was the key to enter the throne room of God. I was desperate for a miracle. As I began to worship God, I quoted this scripture out loud. Next, I repented of my sins and asked God for forgiveness. Then I asked Him to create in me a pure heart and renew a steadfast spirit within me. Finally, I pleaded the blood of Jesus upon me. Immediately I felt the fire of God upon me, and I began ascending into the throne room.

I saw a golden throne with God sitting upon it. I could not make out His face because it was full of this glorious light. He was dressed in white, and His feet were a golden bronze color. I saw some steps below the throne. Then I turned to the sides of the room and seen hundreds of angels on the sides of the room. The room itself is indescribable because I have never seen a room like this before. The walls seemed to look a translucent green color. I threw myself in front of His throne, and I began to speak my decrees for me and others until I fell into a sleepy trance. Then I saw myself descending past the stars, past the clouds, back into my room.

FLAMING ARROWS

Flaming arrows is one of the first visions that I have seen. One day, I was worshipping, and the glory of God pinned me to the floor. I could only turn my head sideways. God took me into the heavenlies. Then I noticed a rider who I couldn't make out who he was. He was sitting on a brown horse with golden wings. Then God showed me a big bow and shooting arrows. I was amazed because I never saw anything like this before. This bow was laying horizontally or sideways and shooting arrows. The bow and arrows were a golden color almost orange. The Lord spoke to me that He was releasing these arrows against my enemies. He said, "As long as you stay in the Spirit, I will release my flaming arrows at your enemies."

After the vision ended, I went to the Bible and began to search for golden arrows but couldn't find it. So a few hours later, I was reading through Psalms and realized that the arrows weren't golden arrows but flaming arrows.

Psalm 7:13 says, "God has deadly weapons in store for those who won't change; he gets his flaming arrows ready!"

GOLDEN SCROLL

On September 19, 2014, I was praying to God early in the morning. I was preparing to do my weekly prayer call. God began to show me an open heaven with blessings pouring down. Demons were stealing blessings and angels were warring against them to get the blessings back.

I saw angels worshipping God in heaven. There were thousands of angels. I saw hundreds of people praying in their homes and their prayers look like smoke. God showed me what His fire looks like which looks almost golden.

Then God took me into someone's house who was demon possessed. Once the demon was cast out, it appeared as a dark black tall shadow, and a fire angel chased it away from the person. Then God showed me how demons look attached to people. Believers can have demons attached to them. This one man who was a believer had seven short black spirits attached to him on the outside. Once I begin to see these spirits, I started to see them everywhere. God often alerts me to pray for people that I am connected to that has these spirits in their homes. I pray until these spirits flee that person's home.

Next, God took me up in the heavenlies where the stars were. My room faded and I was in the galaxy. He told me to reach out and grab a golden scroll. I grabbed this scroll, and He told me to place it inside my belly. Once I placed this scroll into my stomach, I began to have terrible pains in my chest. No matter how much I rebuked the pain, it would not budge. The pain left in a few hours. Later God revealed to me that He impregnated me with His word. I then realized that other prophets in the Bible had experiences with scrolls: Ezekiel and John who wrote revelation ate scrolls.

THE LORD OF LORDS

On Oct. 23, 2014, I had a vision of Jesus who was sitting on a beautiful white horse in the clouds and was wearing a red cape. He had hundreds of angels behind Him in the clouds. He spoke to me, "Tell them that my glory is coming. My Son is coming soon." I later realized that He was talking about His return or coming back.

I confirmed this vision hours later in Revelation 19:11-16. "Then I saw heaven opened, and there was a white horse. Its rider was called Faithful and True, and he judges and makes war justly. His eyes were like a fiery flame, and on his head were many royal crowns. He has a name written on him that no one knows but he himself. He wore a robe dyed with blood, and his name was called the Word of God. Heaven's armies, wearing fine linen that was white and pure, were following him

on white horses. From his mouth comes a sharp
sword that he will use to strike down the nations.
He is the one who will rule them with an iron rod.
And he is the one who will trample the winepress
of the Almighty God's passionate anger. He has a
name written on his robe and on his thigh: King
of kings and Lord of lords."

PUTTING ON CHRIST

In July 2018, the Lord began to speak to me
about miracles. He said, "Do a seven day fast and
you will have unusual miracles in your ministry."
During this time, another minister that I follow
on social media also heard similar words. I knew
that I was in alignment with what God was releasing in that season. The seven days went by
quickly and were easy for me because God gave
me the grace to fast. As I was preparing to break
the fast on the seventh day, I closed my eyes and
began to pray. As I prayed, I went off into a vision. In the vision, I saw a bloody Jesus Christ.
He had scratches all over His face and a crown of
thorns pressed into his scalp with blood seaming

downward. He locked eyes with me and spat out blood. Chills came over my body, and I began to weep.

My eyes shifted to a nearby road, and I saw people of different diversities marching down into town. As I turned to look back at Jesus, he threw a golden sheet at me which pushed me a couple of feet. I looked down and was amazed. I had the bloody scraped up skin of Jesus Christ on my skin. At that moment, Glory engulfed me, and I came out of the vision. I was shocked about what I had just witnessed, and immediately, I began to see an increase of miracles happen as I prayed for someone. It took me a couple of months to testify of this encounter without breaking down and weeping. I got a deeper revelation of putting on Christ (Galatians 3:27).

I had several visitations since then, and each one has changed my life or brought me into a higher dimension with the Lord. After I started walking in the gift of prophecy for a while, the Lord dealt with me about putting the title, "Prophetess," in front of my name. For two weeks, I wrestled internally with the Holy Spirit. "God, please don't make me do this. What will people think?" The Lord was stern, "I called you. You know what you must do!" Finally, I yielded my will to His, and I stepped out. I put Prophetess on my social media networks. Over time, the Holy Spirit began to train me on how to walk uprightly before Him. He gave me a list of instructions that I must do: Fast weekly and take daily communion. He gave me a list of twenty-one books to write and anointed me to write at an accelerated pace.

After two years of faithfully walking in the gift of prophecy, the Lord called me off my job at the hospital into full-time ministry. It was difficult at first because I had to build my faith up to depend on Him not a job at the hospital. I remember getting terminated and cried, "Lord, I'm a single mother with two children. What am I going to do?" The Lord responded, "You are now in the prophetic office. Go back to church. You are going to work the altar and lay hands." I didn't want to hear this. I wanted to work at the hospital, and I didn't want to lay hands on anyone. I thought that I had been in the prophetic office because I prophesied all the time. Now I knew that I was without a shadow of a doubt because God validated it. Once again, God had to get that stubborn streak out of my heart. I obeyed the instructions of the Lord, and He ordered my steps to a church where a pastor was praying for a prophet to serve at his church. The Lord sent me there. Immediately, the pastor knew who I was. I was quickly elevated or promoted in various church responsibilities.

The Lord had me studying about the prophets in the Bible, and He wanted me to start teaching others. I started a series, "The Making of A Prophet," on YouTube and periscope. The broadcast grew as well as my social media following. Over time, the Lord began to increase the prophetic anointing upon my life as I got closer to Him, took training, read books, and received impartation from my spiritual leaders.

CHAPTER THREE

Can Women Preach the Gospel?

Imagine being shut down and being told that you can't preach because you are a woman. Imagine being frustrated because there is a call on your life, but you are prohibited from walking in your call. Women face hindrances daily all over the world. There is an attack of hell against women, and it must be stopped. In many cultures, women are limited in various ways. Some women aren't allowed to drive, get an education, vote, or work outside of the home. Women in these cultures are viewed as property of their husbands and just expected to bear children and do domestic duties. If a woman becomes a widow in these cultures, she may experience great hardship. Some of these women do not have a voice and aren't taken seriously when they express their concerns. In North America, where I'm from, women have more rights and sometimes take more domineering roles.

In ministry, I have been persecuted because I'm a woman. Many men have approached me and told me that I am not supposed to be preaching the gospel of Jesus Christ. They were serious and they trolled my videos or put derogatory comments on my social media pages. They called me a false prophet because they don't believe in women preachers. They took scriptures from the Bible and told me that I was in error. They failed to realize that took the scriptures out of context because they didn't consider the time frame of the text, the overall chapter, and why the text was written. Let's explore the verses these men love to use against women preachers. We will see how they take the verses out of context.

An old mentor of mines told me repeatedly, "Line by line. Precept by precept. The Bible is just like a long letter." He lectured me on how to study the Bible to ensure that I wouldn't take these out of context. When something is taking out of context that means to misconstrue or twist the meaning of its original intent or purposes.

1 Corinthians 14:34 (KJV) says, "Let your women keep silence in the churches: for it is not permitted unto them to speak; but they are commanded to be under obedience as also saith the law."

When someone just reads this scripture without reading the rest of the chapter, they will automatically assume that women should just be silent in churches or not preach. That is dangerous because it allows a spirit of religion to creep in and leads to doctrinal error. Let's look at another Bible translation of the same scripture to get a greater insight.

1 Corinthians 14:34 (EXB) says, "·women [or wives] should keep quiet in the ·church meetings [churches; assemblies; C THE CONTEXT HERE MAY BE THE EVALUATION OF PROPHECY (v. 29), RATHER THAN GENERAL WORSHIP (where women presumably could speak; see 11:2–16)]. [L For] They are not allowed to speak, but they must ·yield to this rule [or be in submission; or keep their ordered place] as the law says [C perhaps Gen. 3:16, or a nonbiblical Jewish tradition]."

This is the Expanded Bible translation. Notice that this scripture is speaking of prophecy not general worship. 1 Corinthians 14 is taking about prophecy. Imagine if the preacher is ministering in front of a congregation and someone stands up in the middle of their sermon and starts prophesying. This is the reason why Apostle Paul the author of 1st and 2nd Corinthians wrote this scripture. There were many women who were acting disorderly and prophesying all over the place. God is not the author of confusion (1 Corinthians 14:33). Notice that 1 Corinthians 14:33 which mentions confusion is right before verse 34 which speaks of women being silent in the church.

In the prophetic, there must order. Let 2 or 3 prophets speak and the others judge (1 Corinthians 14:29). Notice in 1 Corinthians 14:29, that it is giving us structure to abide by and still talking about prophecy. Again, the whole chapter of 1 Corinthians 14 is talking mostly about prophecy. There must be order because people operating in the wrong spirit will disrupt the flow of the Holy Spirit. If twenty or thirty people want to prophesy in a service, it could get very chaotic. Let's look at two more scriptures that people like to use against women preachers.

1 Timothy 2:11-12 (KJV) says, "Let the WOMAN learn in silence with all subjection. But I suffer not a woman to teach, nor to USURP AUTHORITY over the man, but to be in silence."

When you first look at these scriptures it appears that women aren't allowed to teach however we must do deeper level of research to make sure that we don't take these scriptures out of context. Notice in verse 11 it says 'woman' and not women.

It's singular, not plural. Apostle Paul, the author of 1st and 2nd Timothy, might be mentioning a specific woman without saying her name. He wasn't talking to all women. There is always that one person that Satan sends to cause distractions or hinder the move of God in our services.

Apostle Paul was writing a letter to his spiritual son Timothy. In 1 Timothy 1, there were a lot of false teachers in Ephesus. Some of these false teachers went to some of these congregations and spread their false teachings. Apostle Paul warned Timothy (1 Timothy 3-11) about false doctrine.

1 Timothy 2 mentions authority. God never created women to domineer over men. God created women to submit to men especially wives to submit to their husbands (1 Timothy 2:13). That's why Apostle Paul mentions God creating Adam before He created Eve. Apostle Paul was discussing the attributes of women here in these scriptures. He wanted women to learn with an attitude of submission and not an attitude of unruliness.

Now you can see the importance of reading the entire chapter of the Bible or even reading several chapters of it before taking one verse. When we neglect to do so, we can fall into error and take scriptures out of context. In summary, women can preach the gospel of Jesus Christ. Let's explore some women in the Bible that God used powerfully.

CHAPTER FOUR

Women That God Used in the Bible

Many people feel like God can't use them because of their past. I wasn't always a saint. I have always been transparent about what God delivered me from to show people the redemptive power of God. I was an exotic dancer and a Buddhist when I was in the world. Once I even backslid, but I repented and received another chance from the Lord. Now, I'm on fire for God, and I know He is real because I feel His presence every day. God uses me in signs, miracles, and wonders. I have witnessed many miracles in my ministry. You may have a horrible past, but God can still use you. Many women are discriminated against because of their backgrounds, appearance, physical strength, social economic status, and more. I understand how that feels because some people have told me that they don't like the way I look. Their opinions doesn't stop God from using me, and people's opinions will not stop God from using you either.

Some people feel that God can't use women. God used various women throughout the Bible. God used a lady name Rahab (Joshua 2). She was a prostitute. Some people feel like she was the least likely person that God should've used because of who she was, but God had a plan for her. God has a plan for your life as well. Rahab hid the two spies in her home when men from her country sought to kill them. She received the spies with peace (Hebrews 11:31; James 2:25). Rahab played an essential part because she helped the children of the Israelites in their process of receiving their promised land. Rahab is remembered in the hall of faith (Hebrews 11:31) and is a part of Jesus' genealogy (Matthew 1:5).

God used Mary, the mother of Jesus. She had the privilege of carrying and birthing the Messiah which was a huge responsibility to carry God in the Flesh in her womb (John 1:1,14). She found favor in the sight of God (Luke 1:28). She will be forever known as the Virgin Mary or the mother of Jesus. Imagine how much favor you will have with God as you walk uprightly. God wants to use you to make history and impact the world around you for His Glory!

God used the woman at the well in Samaria (John 4:1-42). During this time, people felt like it was a waste of time to educate women which is why Jesus' disciples got mad when they saw Him talking to her (John 4:27). They were surprised to see Him take time out of His schedule and witness unto her. You may have been rejected, but God will always make time for you just like the woman at the well. Some of your spectators may not understand why the hand of the Lord is upon your life, but you are important to Him like this woman in Samaria. She had five husbands, and Jesus Christ had a word of knowledge concerning her. You may have sinned and felt like nothing good will ever come out of your life, but one encounter with God will turn your life into a life of purpose. After their conversation, she went back home to tell everybody about Jesus Christ. She was a woman evangelist. God will use you as well to spread the gospel of His Son Jesus.

Imagine losing everything like your family, sense of security, joy, happiness, etc. Will you give up? Many people do but not Ruth. God used her because of her determination and faithfulness. She had a prominent position because she was a part of the genealogy of Jesus Christ. She was a widow and considered to be at the bottom of the socioeconomic scale. She had to work in the field to take care of her mother-in-law and herself. Many people would've looked down on her, but God caused a man named Boaz to favor her. She went from working in the fields to owning the fields. She was counted in by God. Many people may have counted you out, but God counted you in like He did Ruth. God will use you to be a sign of His restoration and goodness just as He did with Ruth.

God used Esther in the Bible. Esther was a Queen that came from small beginnings. She replaced Queen Vashti who disobeyed the King. Esther didn't want to tell anyone of her past because her mentor, or uncle Mordecai, instructed her not too. She sacrificed herself for her people, the Jews, by approaching King Xerxes unannounced. She fasted and put her life on the line. Her bravery paid off, and her people were delivered from the plans of wicked Haman. You may come from small beginnings just like Esther, but as you remain faithful, God will open doors and cause people of influence to notice you. You are someone's replacement because they aren't walking uprightly before God. God will use you powerfully to set the captives free! Do not despise small beginnings (Zechariah 4:10)!

God used Junia, a woman apostle, in scripture (Romans 16:7). Many people feel like women can't be an apostle, but they fail to realize that God can use whomever He chooses. There is no gender distinction in the five-fold offices. When you look at Ephesians 4:8-12, when Jesus appointed the five-fold offices, He didn't specify that only men could fill these offices. The scripture says, "He gave some apostles..." 'Some' includes everyone from all walks of life. 'Some' includes men and women. How many women out there that are really apostles or prophets, but their leaders shut down their gift and ordained them as an evangelist, deaconess, or an elder because they believe that God can't use women in specific roles?

Now that we have covered that women can preach the gospel and how God can use women let's discuss the warfare women go through!

CHAPTER FIVE

The Warfare Against Women

Most of the churches are filled with more women. Since some men have rejected their calling, God sees faithful women who will respond 'yes' to the call. God is raising up more women to do great things for His Glory! Women in North America are blessed compared to women in some foreign lands. In North America, we have the right to vote, receive an education, and lots of equality laws are in place to cut back on discrimination.

However, women in North America and all over the world go through warfare or demonic attacks. Whenever there is purpose and greatness inside of you, the devil will try his best to discourage you and prevent you from walking in your assignment.

Women are called to do more than look cute, get married, have children, and perform domestic tasks. There is nothing wrong with these things, but for some women, God has placed a yearning in their spirit to want more in life. Women are called to be game changers because they have a purpose in life. However, some women haven't discovered their purpose yet and die without ever fulfilling it. Don't let that be your story! God placed you on this earth for a reason. Now, ask Him, "Lord, what is my purpose in life?" You may hear Him speak or He may reveal it to you in time, but God has a purpose for you.

When He created you, there was an agenda in mind. He decided your nationality, your appearance, your strengths, and your weaknesses. Yes! God did all of this because He created you to be a part of His master plan. When God created you,

He created a masterpiece, or a piece of beautiful artwork set aside for His use. We are God's handiwork (Ephesians 2:10). God created you to reach certain people that He is calling you too. You were designed to do great exploits for God. That's why the devil is fighting you so hard!

I'm a wife, mother, daughter, sister, spiritual daughter, mentor, spiritual mother, Publisher, Author, editor, entrepreneur, prophet, intercessor, and more. I have many different roles, yet I am fulfilling the call upon my life and you can too. There were many times the devil attacked me because people were being delivered, healed, and saved. At the right moment, the Holy Spirit said, "You can't quit because that's what the devil wants. Try again. Keep on pressing! Keep fighting! My promises will come to pass in your life! I'm working things out on your behalf." When I heard these words in prayer, I was renewed and gained the strength to keep fighting the good fight of faith. Receive the very same words for yourself to keep on pushing past the warfare. Making less money and not being heard is some warfare women encounter.

MAKING LESS MONEY

Every day, women all around the world make less money than men. They are working in the same position for the same amount of hours, but some men get paid more which is unjust. This practice has been going on for years, and more wickedness is being exposed. If you are going through warfare on your job and being mistreated, hang tight because vindication is coming for you. God specializes in righting wrongs. He stands for justice. He loves what is right and fair.

Psalm 33:5 says, "He loveth righteousness and judgment: the earth is full of the goodness of the Lord."

HAVING NO VOICE

Some women don't have a voice and when they speak their opinions aren't respected nor valued which can be very frustrating. God understands how it feels to speak, and no one is listening. He has been sending prophets since the beginning of time to proclaim the arrival of His Son, but people refused to listen. They were stiff-necked and rebellious. Keep crying out and speak, "Thus saith the Lord!" Someone is listening. You are watering and planting seeds of the gospel (1 Corinthians 3:7).

I have witnessed many women's husbands shut their ministry down. Perhaps, it was jealousy or intimidation. When a woman can fulfill her purpose, she is more content. My prayer is that every husband realizes the anointing upon their wife's life and encourage, support, and help push her forward. A husband and wife team are a powerful force to be reckoned with. Teamwork makes the dream work. Most wives are their husband's prophet and intercessor. Men should listen to their wives because God allowed that man to find his good thing (Proverbs 18:22).

CHAPTER SIX

Huldah

The meaning of Huldah is 'weasel.' Weasels are skilled hunters and relentless killers. They aren't afraid to take down prey that is bigger than them. Prophets need to be like the weasel: courageous and take out the enemy. We can't be afraid of those mountains that are set before us or the severity of the demonic attacks. Prophets have to be snipers in the spirit and do damage to the enemy's camp.

Huldah was a prophetess that was sought after (2 Kings 22:13-14). Her husband was Shallum who kept up with the King's wardrobe. We know more about her husband than we do her. We can trace Shallum's lineage but not hers. We can read about her story in 2 Kings 22:14-20. The high priest, royal secretary, and some of the King's servants went to inquire of the Lord due to finding a book of teachings about God's laws or Torah. When the King heard what was in the Torah, he tore his clothes because he realized that everyone wasn't obeying God's commandments and ordered his servants to seek a word from the prophet.

When you are a prophet, your gift will cause you to be sought out just like Huldah. Huldah gave the word of the Lord, and it caused the people's hearts to return unto God. True prophets always point people back to Jesus Christ. She received two words of knowledge.

1) That a man who was a King sent these men to seek a word from the Lord.

2) That the King tore his clothes, repented, and cried in God's presence.

Some prophets have a strong grace for the word of knowledge. The closer you become to Jesus, the stronger the gift. Huldah's prophecy exposed the previous sins of idolatry and disobedience. True prophets of God expose sin. They aren't afraid to call it out. This prophecy showed the mercy of God because the King would be spared of witnessing the pending judgment. God promised him that it would happen after he was dead. Prophets extend the mercy of God to the broken, and they remind people of His promises.

Huldah's prophecy resulted in reformation (2 Kings 23). All the people gathered together to hear the laws of God being read. They repented and promised to obey the word of God. King Josiah destroyed all the high places of Idol worship and commanded everyone to celebrate Passover. God wants you to be an instrument of righteousness that will cause a change in this earth.

Step out prophet and allow God to fill your mouth with His words. The prophetic word can bring life to dead things. The prophetic word will cause repentance and bring heaven down to earth. Be bold like Huldah was. Don't get intimidated by the faces of men. Don't shrink back when the enemy launches an attack. God is with you, prophet. Get ready because you have been faithful, and God will cause your gift to be sought after. The gifting on your life will be in demand.

CHAPTER SEVEN

Deborah

The name Deborah means bee. Bees are hard workers, and they play an essential part in our ecosystem. They help germinate plants and flowers by spreading pollen. They also make honey which provides a food source for humans, insects, and animals. Prophets must be hard workers, and they play an important part in the body of Christ. The church is founded on the apostles and prophets (Ephesians 2:20). The prophets are the eyes and the mouth of the body of Christ;

that's why they are so vital, just like bees are to our ecosystem.

Deborah was a prophetess that was well respected in her day. We can read about her story in Judges 4. When you walk uprightly in the prophetic office, God will bestow honor upon you. People know that if you receive a prophet and bless them, then they will receive the prophet's rewards (Matthew 10:41). There was a lot of evil and corruption going on, so God raised up Deborah to be a voice. Whenever there is chaos, God will raise up prophets to be a voice in the land. God needs messengers to speak His word to cause people's hearts to return unto Him. The Lord chose Deborah as His judge to be a leader among His people. True prophets are chosen by God, not self-appointed.

Deborah was the wife of Lapidoth. She would sit underneath the palm tree every day, and people began to seek her every day for judgment or to settle their disputes. Deborah had wisdom from God which caused her to be able to give Godly counsel. Prophets need the wisdom of God to instruct people in righteousness and in the will of God. Many people will come to prophets with various challenges, but it takes a yielded prophet to speak the heart and mind of God for a person's life.

Prophets aren't intimidated by the enemy or his threats. Deborah prophesied the wicked Sisera's downfall. Sisera was cruel and had 900 iron chariots. The Israelites cried out to God, and prophetess Deborah was able to discern the timing of the Lord. Prophets must be sensitive to God's timing because everything will fall into place. Once I was planning a conference, and nothing was working out. The Lord gave me dates, but I changed them to accommodate someone's schedule. I had a hard time finding a venue, so I changed my dates to what I heard originally. Once I changed the dates, I found a venue in no time. Deborah was able to discern when to attack the enemy. She knew how to flow with God because she released a Rhema word or a word in the right season for the right time.

When Deborah began to prophesy, it triggered a set of events. The atmosphere started to shift. The people who were once afraid of Sisera gained strength and courage to gather together and fight him and his army. This prophetic triggered all of heaven to move on the children of Israelites' behalf. Prophets have power and authority in their mouths. There were many times when God filled my mouth with His words, and I began to see the sick healed, demons being cast out, and blessings released. The same way God raised up Deborah in a chaotic time, He will raise you up in this wicked and perverse generation. God will show you how powerful His words are in your mouth. God is calling You for such a time as this!

CHAPTER EIGHT

Isaiah's Wife

Some people assume that if a man is an Apostle then his wife is a prophetess. They slap a title in front of the wife's name even though she may not even function as a prophet. When people place titles in front of people's name or ordain them as something that they aren't then that's dangerous. The prophetic attracts a lot of warfare. I always tell my students that they must be careful with titles because if they don't have the anointing to match that office, then they will deal with prophetic level demons. My spiritual father says, "The prophetic is like a shining light that attracts everything. Some witches are drawn to the prophetic." We see people often with titles but no anointing. Some people that are ordained as prophets can't even prophesy.

Every day, the enemy is fighting God's prophets by trying to discourage, kill them, or destroy their ministries. I had many attacks. I had witches try to curse and kill me. A witch came to one of my conferences trying to disrupt it, but she couldn't stop anything. Later, God made sure she faced repercussions. Another witch attempted to destroy my ministry by going around harassing everyone that was connected to me. Once, a witch astral projected into my room and tried to snatch my spirit out of my body. Another time, a witch tried to physically choke me in the spirit realm. Each time, God protected me. He promised me protection if I stay in His will. God saves His anointed (Psalms 20:6). Spiritual warfare is real, but it also helps us to remain humble. When we face challenges, we know that we need the Lord's help. So, the warfare is designed to keep us in prayer.

We never heard Isaiah's wife prophesy, but we know that she was a prophetess. We can read about Isaiah's wife in Isaiah 8:3. She conceived or gave birth to a son. Prophets can birth out new things in God. When you connect with a prophet, new things will be birthed out. The voice of the Lord makes the calves give birth (Psalm 29:9). A prophetic word can cause God to birth or release new things in your life. God will release things that you have never thought about. You will be amazed to see how God opens up new assignments and opportunities unto you. God has used me to prophesy new things into people's lives. They couldn't see it at first, but they received the prophetic word, and it manifested in their lives.

CHAPTER NINE

Anna

Anna means grace. God gives His prophets grace to do what they are called to do (Romans 12:3). Anna had a strong grace to fast and worship the Lord in the temple. Prophets love to worship God because it ushers His presence into the room or shifts the atmosphere. Prophets love feeling the presence of the Lord because in His presence is the fullness of joy (Psalm 16:11). Prophets draw strength from God because they recognize that He is their source. When I go through trials, I go into worship and rest in the presence of God. I may fall on my knees discouraged but when I get up after being in God's presence, I am renewed and restored.

We can learn a lot from the ministry of Anna by reading about her in Luke 2:36-38. She was the daughter of Phanuel from the tribe of Asher. She had been widowed for eighty-four years. She was older but powerful. Many people feel like God can't use them because of their age. Not true. Anna was in her eighties and God was using her mightily. Her mandate was to worship God day and night. She never left the temple. She created a prophetic atmosphere that a devout man name Simeon was able to prophesy about the Messiah when he saw baby Jesus (Luke 2:33-35). Prophets create prophetic atmospheres and it's easy for someone to prophesy underneath that anointing. When people take my prophetic training, they can prophesy easily because they are under the prophetic anointing.

Imagine how much glory was in the temple because Anna was constantly worshipping God. Worship attracts the presence of God to create a glorious atmosphere. Anna also was a prayer warrior because she prayed day and night. Prophets must pray because that's how we communicate with God. I have witnessed many religions such as Buddhist chant for hours and Muslims praying and fasting for a whole month. However, some Christians struggle in this area. They don't want to fast or pray. When God calls me to fast the results are powerful. I see many miracles take place in the lives of people that I minister to such as deaf ears open, legs grow out evenly, lumps dissolving, crooked limbs straighten, and much more. During my first prayer conference, not too many people came. However, when I did my first prophetic conference, the church was full. Prophets must be passionate about praying because they can tap into the heart and mind of God which is why prophets are great intercessors.

Anna also had a strong gift of the word of knowledge (Luke 2:38) because she knew supernaturally who Joseph, Mary, and Jesus was when she laid eyes upon them as they stood in the temple. Anna began to thank God and spoke about Jesus being the redeemer to everyone that would listen. She wasn't afraid to evangelize or spread the great news of the gospel. We all are called to do the work of an evangelist (2 Timothy 4:5). We must share our faith with others because that blood will be on our hands. One day we will all stand in front of the judgment seat and those souls that weren't witnessed to will flash before our eyes.

Many things will be birthed out in prayer. What we do privately, God will reward us publicly (Matthew 6:6). It's time, prophet, to fast, pray, and worship the Lord as never before. When we fast, we break down strongholds (Isaiah 58:6). When you pray, you get results (Matthew 7:7). The Holy Spirit told me years ago that, "Worship brings in the harvest." When we worship, our blessings locate us in the spirit. We can see the sacrificial lifestyle of a prophet that is required through the ministry of Anna. Your sacrifice is not in vain.

CHAPTER TEN

Miriam

The name Miriam means stubborn. Prophets can be stubborn in their ways, but God knows how to take them through the process of molding them into the image of His Son Jesus. I was always stubborn growing up, but I learned through many trials to yield my agenda and submit to God's will for my life. Miriam was a prophetess and the older sister of Moses. We can learn a lot through the ministry of Miriam. We can see how prophets are called to be a watchman through her. Prophets must keep watch and intercede against the plans of the enemy.

In Exodus 2:4-9, we can witness a younger Miriam. When Miriam was younger, she watched Moses being put into a basket on the Nile River. She followed him along the river and saw Pharaoh's daughter pick him out of the basket. Miriam was watching through the tall grass. God will warn prophets and show them things in advance. As Pharaoh's daughter and her slave girl discovered baby Moses, Miriam approached them and suggested, "Do you want me to find a Hebrew woman to nurse this child?" They agreed. Miriam went and got her own mother to nurse her baby. Moses' mother got paid to care for her own child.

The prophetic anointing creates an economy or generates wealth. Prosperity is connected to the prophetic. Once a pastor became upset with me because he didn't believe it, but it proves to be true in my life and others connected to me. God releases ideas that generate multiple streams of income. As I worship, I get revelation that causes me to prosper in many areas. Miriam's idea created a source of income for her parents which was

God's blessing upon them. God gave them double for their trouble. For months, Moses' parents had to hide him due to the wicked law to kill all male children under the age of two.

After God performed the Red Sea miracle, Miriam took a tambourine, danced, and sang a prophetic song unto the Lord (Exodus 15). Many women began to follow her and sang along. Prophets love to dance and worship the Lord. The word of the Lord filled their mouths in song. God has given me many songs, and as I sing them, others are blessed by them. The song of the Lord is an anointed song for that moment that will set the captives free. She was able to flow prophetically and sing after Moses finished singing. The song of the Lord shifts the atmosphere.

Prophets have the hand of the Lord upon their lives, and they can't do what they want to do. God chastises those who He loves (Hebrews 12:6). He rebukes His prophets when they are out of order. Miriam didn't like Moses' new wife, so she spoke out against her. When God heard this, He was upset and struck her with leprosy (Numbers 12). Since Miriam was a leader, she had to be held accountable by her words. Leaders have great influence and what they say affects many people. If people heard her speaking out against Moses' wife, then they would follow suit and start speaking out against her as well which would result in rebellion in the camp. Prophets must be mindful of what they say because their words carry weight in the spirit and many people honor their words.

We can learn about the ranks of the spirit when we look at the ministry of Miriam. She was a prophet, and she heard God, yet she didn't outrank her brother Moses in the spirit. She was called to serve the vision that God gave Moses. If you are faithful with another man's vision, then God will provide you with your own (Luke 16:12). Many people are operating in rebellion because they are going against their leader and the vision that the Lord gave them. God judged the sons of Korah because of their rebellion and caused the earth to open up to swallow them (Numbers 16:32). Most people are operating in pride because they feel like God speak to them as well. God is a God of order, and He expects us to submit to leadership (Romans 13:1).

CHAPTER ELEVEN

False Prophets

Many people can't distinguish the difference between a true or a false prophet. Some people feel like a false prophet is someone that misses it when they prophesy. That isn't always the case because the person could be a budding prophet or even a presumptuous prophet. Yes, a sign of a false prophet is when their prophecies don't come to pass (Deuteronomy 18:22). However, there were times when God changed His mind about the prophetic word that was given which was the case in Jonah's ministry. Jonah prophesied that in forty days Nineveh would be overthrown, but God changed His mind because the people repented when they heard the prophecy.

There were times when people called me false because they didn't like my appearance. They never listened to me preach or teach. Sometimes, I was called false because the person didn't understand certain manifestations of the Holy Spirit flowing through me. I have done extensive training on this subject matter in, "School of the Prophets: A Curriculum for Success." I have witness people come against major ministers in the body of Christ because they didn't like their ministry and they called them false prophets. Again, just because someone doesn't like a person or agree with them doesn't make them false.

One of the signs of a false prophet is the fruit that they produce (Matthew 7:15-16). We want to produce the fruit of the Holy Spirit. I always teach people about allowing God to develop character in us because if we don't have character, we can easily get into witchcraft. I have witness people come and go in ministry. One of the saddest things I experienced was a woman I used to minister with is now a witch. My heart broke as I grieved over her sins. I kept praying for her until one day the Lord said, "She made her choice. Stop praying for her." I didn't understand why the Lord would tell me such a thing until I read the story of Samuel grieving over Saul. The Lord spoke to him, and he was able to move forward (1 Samuel 16:1). After I received the Lord's counsel and read this story, I was able to release this person in prayer.

Two female prophets were false in scripture: Noadiah and Jezebel. We can read about Noadiah in Nehemiah 6:14. She caused fear in Nehemiah's heart as he was on assignment to rebuild the wall. Noadiah was with Tobiah, Sanballat, and some other prophets whose names aren't mentioned. They did everything that they could to distract, discourage, and torment Nehemiah. They didn't have the character of God (Jesus), and they went against what He was establishing. Whenever you go against the move of God, you are false. True prophets of God are friends of God. True prophets want the will of God done in the earth. Noadiah was being used by the enemy or devil to cause great fear inside Nehemiah. He was so afraid that he and all his workers had to build the wall with a weapon on their hips (Nehemiah 4:17-18). A true prophet of God will pray and encourage you to complete your God-given assignment.

Jezebel was a false prophetess. She was self-appointed because God didn't call her. She called herself. Many people on social media are calling themselves without having an authentic call from God. They feel like being a prophet is a way to make a lot of money, to get famous, or to be more important. Whatever the reason, God didn't send them.

Revelation 2:20 says, "Notwithstanding I have a few things against thee, because thou suffer-est that woman Jezebel, which calleth herself a prophetess, to teach and to seduce my servants to commit fornication, and to eat things sacrificed unto idols."

Jezebel called herself a prophetess. She went against the ways of God. She caused God's peo-ple to stumble by getting entangled in sexual sins and eating forbidden foods. A true prophet of God is going to promote the word of God and upkeep His standards. A true prophet of God is going to encourage you to live Holy. Jezebel massacred the prophets of God (1 Kings 18:13). She had her own prophets: four hundred fifty prophets of Baal and the four hundred prophets of Asherah that ate from her table (1 Kings 18:19). Jezebel took care of her false prophets during the time of famine by making sure they ate well. She was the biggest enemy to Elijah and threatened to kill him when she got word that he slaughtered her prophets (1 Kings 19).

Jezebel had a spirit of seduction. We can see this spirit running rampant today in the body of Christ. Many people can't discern the spirit in operation in an individual. The spirit of seduction will tell you words of flattery and what they will do for you if you connect with them or do something for them. This spirit is dangerous and very crafty. Many people ignore the red flags the Holy Spirit gives and take the bait of listening to the enticing words that puffs up one's ego. Once a pastor wanted to connect with me, and he told me everything that he would do for me if I allowed him too. He made some grand promises, but when I went to bed later that night, I had a dream. In my dream was a mutual person that the pastor and I were associated with. When I woke up from the dream, I felt terrible, and I knew God was telling me not to connect with this person. I shook off the eerie feeling and proceeded with the business transaction.

It was a big mistake. I discovered that the pastor was unfaithful to his wife and was known to have affairs. He was a thorn in my flesh and tried to take over everything that I was building. He was very demanding and belittling. I lost my peace and was stressed out. I had to repent before the Lord and disconnected myself from him. Once I got rid of him, I got my peace back and learned a valuable lesson. Wait on God to open doors and bring the promises to pass in your life. When you wait on God, you won't be so desperate and take the bait of seduction. I was blessed to only have suffered a lack of peace and some hurt feelings. Some people lose much more such as their ministries, families, businesses, etc. The spirit of Jezebel is attacking the prophets of God today. We must be careful because this spirit isn't gender specific and will suck the life out of you.

CHAPTER TWELVE

Queen Mother

When the term, "Queen Mother," is mentioned, many people may think of a queen who is a mother. Also, they may remember the late famous Elizabeth Angela Marguerite Bowes-Lyon who was the wife of King George VI and the mother of Queen Elizabeth II. A queen mother is a woman who is in a high-ranking position or who has an authoritative voice. She could also be the wife of a King or female ruler. Such a woman has a great level of authority and is highly influential. Queen mother is mentioned several times in the scriptures (1 Kings 15:13, 2 Kings 10:13, 2 Chr. 15:16, Jer. 13:18, Jer. 29:2, Dan.5:10). A queen mother can influence the King's decisions, whether good or bad.

1 Kings 21:25 says, "There was no one like Ahab who ·had chosen so often [L sold himself] to do ·what the Lord said was wrong [L evil in the eyes/sight of the Lord], ·because his wife Jezebel INFLUENCED him to do evil [urged on by his wife Jezebel]."

Asa was a King who did right in the sight of God. He removed the Sodomites or the male temple prostitutes out of the land. He removed the Queen mother, Maacah, because she worshiped idols and made a pole to Asherah, an ancient goddess.

1 Kings 15:11-13 (EXB) says, "Asa did what ·the Lord said was right [L was right in the eyes/ sight of the Lord], as his ·ancestor [L father] David had done. He ·forced the male prostitutes at the worship places to leave the country [expelled/ banished the male cult prostitutes from the land; 14:24]. He also took away the idols that his

·ancestors [fathers] had made. His ·grandmother [mother; ancestor] Maacah had made a ·terrible [obscene; repulsive; abominable] Asherah ·idol [pole; 14:15], so Asa removed her from being QUEEN MOTHER. He cut down ·that idol [her obscene/repulsive/abominable image/pole] and burned it in the Kidron Valley."

Asa knew that he had to cut off Maacah's influence because she would've caused others to worship Asherah. He destroyed the demonic pole that she made by burning it in the valley of Kidron. True prophets of God must arise and cut off the enemy's access to people's lives. We must send the fire of God upon the enemy's camp to burn up wickedness. If we aren't on the offensive or actively attacking the enemy before he attacks us, then we will be less effective. John the Baptist's ministry was destroyed because of the QUEEN MOTHER.

In Matthew 14:1-12, John the Baptist called out King Herod's sin. He said, "It's unlawful to marry the wife of your brother, Philip." Herodias was a QUEEN MOTHER. She used her influence to seduce her husband into killing John the

Baptist. It was Herodias, who asked her daughter to dance seductively before the King and his guests. The King was so pleased that he said, "I will give you anything that you want." The daughter replied, "Give me the head of John the Baptist on a platter." When the wrong woman is in position, she will destroy God's servants, just like Herodias did to John the Baptist. Allow God to work on your character, transforming you into the image of Jesus Christ so God can place you in positions of great authority and influence. When God's daughters do their part, God will do His part. God will remove the wicked QUEEN MOTHER in high positions and replace them with His women prophets.

About The Author

Kimberly Moses started off her ministry as Kimberly Hargraves. She is highly sought after as a prophetic voice, intercessor and prolific author. There is no doubt that she has a global mandate on her life to serve the nations of the world by spreading the Gospel of Jesus Christ. She has a quickly expanding worldwide healing and deliverance ministry. Kimberly Moses wears many hats to fulfill the call God has placed on her life as an entrepreneur over several businesses including her own personal brand Rejoice Essentials which promotes the Gospel of Jesus Christ.

She also serves as a life coach and mentor to many women. She is also the loving mother of two wonderful children. She is married to Tron. Kimberly has dedicated her life to the work of ministry and to serve others under the call God has placed over her life. Kimberly currently resides in South Carolina.

She is a very anointed woman of God who signs, miracles and wonders follow. The miraculous and

incessant testimonies attributed to her ministry
are incalculable, with many reporting physical
and mental healing, financial breakthroughs,
debt cancellations and other favorable outcomes.
She is known across the globe as a servant who
truly labors on behalf of God's people through
intercession.

She is the author of The Following:

*"Overcoming Difficult Life Experiences with
Scriptures and Prayers"*
"Overcoming Emotions with Prayers"
"Daily Prayers That Bring Changes"
"In Right Standing,"
"Obedience Is Key,"
*"Prayers That Break The Yoke Of The Enemy:
A Book Of Declarations,"*
*"Prayers That Demolish Demonic Strongholds: A
Book Of Declarations,"*
*"Work Smarter. Not Harder. A Book Of
Declarations For The Workforce,"*
"Set The Captives Free: A Book Of Deliverance."
"Pray More Challenge"
"Walk By Faith: A Daily Devotional"

"Empowering The New Me: Fifty Tips To Becoming A Godly Woman"

"School of the Prophets: A Curriculum For Success"

"8 Keys To Accessing The Supernatural"

"Conquering The Mind: A Daily Devotional"

"Enhancing The Prophetic In You"

"The ABCs of The Prophetic: Prophetic Characteristics"

"Wisdom Is The Principal Thing: A Daily Devotional"

"It Cost Me Everything"

You can find more about Kimberly at www.kimberlyhargraves.com

Index

A

B

Printed in Great Britain
by Amazon